TARGET
YOUR
PASSION

Simple Guide to
Seniors' Successful 2nd Careers

Joy D. Holland

WESTBOW
PRESS®
A DIVISION OF THOMAS NELSON
& ZONDERVAN

WestBow Press books may be ordered through booksellers or by contacting:

WestBow Press
A Division of Thomas Nelson & Zondervan
1663 Liberty Drive
Bloomington, IN 47403
www.westbowpress.com
844-714-3454

ISBN: 978-1-6642-2712-5 (sc)
ISBN: 978-1-6642-2713-2 (hc)
ISBN: 978-1-6642-2711-8 (e)

Library of Congress Control Number: 2021904854

Print information available on the last page.

WestBow Press rev. date: 3/17/2021

Contents

Dedication vii

Introduction ix

1. Where am I? 1

2. The Proverbial "Rut" and how we got there... 9

3. What can I do about it? 21

4. What am I good at doing, what do I
   love to do? 29

5. How can I turn this into a second
   career? ...or do I even want one? 37

6. The Rest of the Story 47

Conclusion...55

About the author 63

Dedication

The idea for this book started at a writer's seminar. A young author made a presentation for a "How to..." for young people. The subject of her book is irrelevant; but as she was speaking, the thought came to me to do a "How to..." for seniors. We've all needed guidance throughout our lives for various reasons so, why not for us after retirement.

So, I would like to dedicate this book to all the seniors who found themselves at loose ends around their retirement years. The hope is that some will find direction or some small help within these pages, based on the stories of the people's lives. I'd love to know that this has become a resource for others.

Introduction

Once upon a time... isn't that how stories begin? Well, heading into retirement is no story. It's reality for all of us, regardless of the circumstances, harder on some than on others. No one really knows how to plan for life after a career or work. We're taught to save for retirement (if we can). We're not taught what to do with ourselves once our days become endless, with nothing more to do, nothing more for us to feel useful. Not everyone has the opportunity to travel on long vacations, to play 36 holes every week or "shop till you drop."

So, what are we to do? Not everyone is able to decide how to spend their remaining time but then, not everyone wants to do that. Some choose to do as little as possible which is fine. Others need to have something to do and can develop their own plans for the future. Some would like to make their plans but don't have the direction. This book is written for these folks.

Here, you'll read about five people who found themselves in this place, needing to plan but not really knowing how. Step by step each one was able make their plans, implement them and find fulfilment in their lives.

Where am I?

Deprived of meaningful work, men and women lose their reason for existence; they go stark, raving mad.

– FYODOR DOSTOEVSKY

I've heard that if you love what you do, you'll never work a day in your life. Do what you love!? BUT, what is it?! Our heart's desire is to do something meaningful, to make a contribution, and make our mark in the world.

At the end of our chosen careers, regardless of how they were chosen, we no longer consider ourselves as useless as those people did, who were in the workforce before us. We are no longer 'the elderly.' We are an active, vibrant group of senior citizens whose loves, energetic and creative lives don't stop with our careers at retirement. We're unable to just sit and do nothing after fifty or sixty years of making a living, having a career and being busy raising a family. Our passion doesn't necessarily include the need to complement our income, nor does it need to consume every spare moment of our time. And it doesn't need to encompass any of what we had done in our careers, although it might. We can continue to live our lives, this time on <u>our own terms</u>.

Many of us were clear about what we wanted for a career. Some of us went to school to get a degree so that we could pursue the career choice we made. Some of us didn't get further education but fell into the first path that came to us. Regardless, we worked diligently throughout our lives and believed we had made a difference – or not. At times our profession became tedious; so, we either persevered or changed companies and/or locations. Sometimes we changed companies so that we could advance in our chosen field. So many of us fell into a job, and/or a career path and just stayed with it because it was safe.

It was what we knew best at the time. Many of us didn't know much about ourselves except what was presented to us as a guide for our lives, a guide which we may or may not have followed. Some of us chose a career path we followed, some of us changed paths, sometimes several times.

We knew we needed to support ourselves and perhaps a family, or even an extended family. As time went on we got into a rut. We worked, we vacationed, we bought and sold our own homes, cars, furniture, as time ebbed and flowed by us. In short, we lived our lives. Life was familiar, and familiarity was comfortable. Some of us developed hobbies, some did not. We were too busy making a living to make a life. What did we leave in the background? Because it truly is in the background, it wasn't lost completely.

Now then, now is the time for retrospection – navel-gazing if you will.

- What am I going to do?
- Where am I headed now?
- Do I know?
- Do I have any ideas?
- Any clues?

How about asking and answering the following questions for yourself:

- Am I in a rut?
- How did I get here? Or does it even matter?
- What can I do about it?
- What am I good at doing?
- What do I love to do?
- How can I turn it into a part/full time second career?

- What does it require?
- Do I even WANT a second career – or do I just want a hobby?

For most of us, we've spent our entire adult lives asking these questions in helping to guide others - siblings, our children, students, employees. Isn't it about time for us to start focusing inward instead of outward? What will happen to us if we don't? Statistics prove that those who retire into a rocking chair fare very poorly. Their quality of life is not optimum, and their lives are shortened by boredom, poor health or both. What a shameful loss! We still have so much more to give!

Far too few of us have the resources to live the life of retirement utopia. Exotic cars, huge homes, exclusive restaurants, designer fashions, travel, unlimited vacations to faraway places;

yes, that would be wonderful, but really. Is that practical – or even possible!?

How would YOU like to spend the rest of YOUR life? Seriously. What would you do to get to where you want to go… or do you even know?

The Proverbial "Rut" and how we got there…

Many people are in a rut and
a rut is nothing but a grave -
with both ends kicked out.

- VANCE HAVNER

What do we do when we find ourselves at the end of when the working/corporate world would consider us no longer useful, or when we've had enough of the daily grind? Do we just shrink back from life and spend the rest of our lives in the recliner or rocking chair and watch the world pass us by, or spend time in front of the TV or computer? OR, do we start looking for our future?

- Get a hobby?
- Get reacquainted with our family?
- Join a club?
- Organize a neighborhood watch?
- Work for a political party?
- Work with a church group? Volunteer for a ministry?

What do we do if we need to supplement what we've managed to save IF we've managed to save anything at all? Sometimes we found ourselves in a place we knew that saving for our future would have caused some serious hardships for our present. We all know that Social Security and Medicare are not adequate to sustain our lives at retirement.

What will you do?

The following are some examples of people who determined that the lemons life handed them would be turned into lemonade. They reached inside themselves and found resources they didn't know they had and made their lives happier, more content and yes, even more productive.

Gloria

Gloria had worked for the bank for her entire life. She'd gotten her job right out of high school and settled completely into the culture. She held several positions and worked her way up to bank manager. She knew that her job was always going to be secure. The day she turned fifty-five she realized that her life had all but passed her by. Somehow, it was a stunning revelation. Sure, she'd gotten married and had the requisite career, the proverbial home with the white picket fence, 2.5 kids, two dogs and a cat. Between herself and her husband, they had managed to save and invest for a comfortable retirement.

Her son and daughter were grown with families and careers of their own and didn't have much time for their parents. Just after he retired Gloria's husband, Matt, suffered a massive stroke which left him almost completely incapacitated and unable to care for himself, let alone travel as they had planned before the kids came along. Gloria was in a rut, caring for the man she loved and getting ready to retire. What was she going to do?

Ted

Ted was a college graduate, top of his class in his chosen field of business. He'd worked for a few different corporations and climbed the ladder of success higher within each new position, until he got almost to the top. Working to provide for his family, he had neglected time with them. Because his wife, the love of his life, had gotten tired of living with a workaholic; she and the kids had left him to find companionship, to make a family elsewhere. Heartbroken, Ted refused to look for another relationship. At the age of fifty-seven, he had gotten a devastating diagnosis. He'd been in the peak of health all his life, but his genes had played a cruel trick on him. In a few short years, Ted was destined to spend the rest of his life in a wheelchair. Active all his life, he became more and more angry, as though he was going to be in a rut with no place else to go.

Maggie

Maggie was a single mom whose only child, a daughter, had left home to begin her own life. Stephie had been able to earn a scholarship to one of the most prestigious universities in her home state and was well on her way to building her own life.

Maggie had been self-employed as a housekeeper raising her daughter, but as she had gotten older, her work had begun to take its toll on her body. She was unable to handle the equipment necessary to do the job as well because her back had started to give her problems. Uneducated, Maggie found herself in a rut.

Chris

Chris was a typical contractor for a home construction company. He loved his work and being out in the weather, for him, was exhilarating. He had risen from carpenter to managing his own crew. Worn out from all the hard work he had done by the time he had decided to retire, Chris was now ready to just relax and unwind; spend time getting to know his wife better. Their kids had families of their own, and he looked forward to finding himself too. After a couple of months, he started to have "cabin fever" and wanted to find something to do. His wife was in complete agreement. Bored, Chris found himself in a rut of daily routine.

Jessie

At the age of sixty, Jessie found herself divorced and alone after decades of being a wife and mother who worked odd jobs to keep the family together. Her husband was sent from one state or country to another, and being wife and mother in a military family whose main breadwinner was an enlistee – not an officer – was no picnic. Raising a family with few resources was hard; especially since her husband spent whatever he wanted for whatever he wanted, usually for alcohol and other women – you know, the sad kind of women who sell themselves for services.

Not only that, but she had a history of being abused by both her father and her husband. She had gotten only a high school education and not a lot of experience with each of the various jobs she worked, mostly for minimum wages. There were a lot of different experiences but not enough on which to lean. To say the least: she was terrified of being alone and hadn't any support from her family, all of whom lived out of state.

What do these five people have in common? They have arrived at the doorstep of an unknown future and now must make the choice to make lemonade out of lemons – or not. One of them has a comfortable retirement package available even though spousal medical bills will deplete it; another's retirement would be eaten up with medical bills, the third had no retirement at all, the fourth was simply looking to add a little something to his existence and the fifth one... well, what resources could she find – especially those within herself? What were any of them going to do?

What can I do about it?

Always fall in with what you're asked to accept. Take what is given and make it over your way. My aim in life has always been to hold my own with whatever's going. Not against: with.

– ROBERT FROST

The key to change... is to let go of fear.

– ROSANNE CASH

Not too many of us get to live the "happily ever after" of the hopes and dreams from our childhood. Most of us find ourselves in one or another of those kinds of situations. Like many of the rest of us; Gloria, Ted, Maggie, Chris and Jessie had some really difficult choices to make. Not one of them had any idea of where to begin. The first thing each of them did, after taking time to bemoan their future, was to face it and take stock of the situation in which they found themselves. They then listed their strengths and weaknesses, what they loved (and didn't) and what they could do; and whether it was something they even wanted to do.

As we all need to do, each of these five took time to grieve the various states they found themselves in, to let the negativity go. They learned to face the facts and tried to deal with what life had handed them in a productive way. They were able, and willing, to take a good hard look at their lives and eliminate the things that no longer mattered or were no longer relevant. As they worked at introspection, they wrote down what seemed to be making a promise toward a better future. At first, there was little in the way of spontaneity unless it was a thought that came suddenly from their sub-conscious. Sometimes, just sometimes, these thoughts could hold the key to delight for the future.

Gloria

Gloria knew she had some time to develop feasible plans for her future with Matt, however long that might be. She wanted to stay busy but distracted from some of the drama of her life. Matt could offer some suggestions, which he did to encourage her; but he wasn't able to do much else. In the end, she knew that taking care of Matt was her main priority, along with whatever assistance they both might need; and she knew she would need to drop everything she was doing at a moment's notice.

Ted

Ted, on the other hand, was angry, so very angry. He felt cheated, and probably rightly so; but that made no difference. His future was quite clear. He was no longer going to be able to be an active contender in his favorite spare time sport of golf, of that he knew without a doubt. So. He had to decide to plan what was, hopefully, going to be a good future. Reluctantly, he began his search. What kind of a life was he going to have?

Maggie

Maggie was nearly at a complete loss. Her occupation was no longer available because of her health. She was organized and more than competent in her chosen career and was able to help her clients organize their homes to the best advantage. She had developed special products that safely cleaned a variety of surfaces. She knew how to buzz through their homes and do a good job. But were her specialized skills needed now that she was older?

Chris

Chris had done a few things between contracts and was still able-bodied, however slow he might be. He was good with his hands and a meticulous wood-worker. He remembered the toys he made for his kids when they were small, and the thought made him smile. Come to think about it, he believed he still had the tools he had used stored either in his garage or in the basement.

Jessie

Jessie had a variety of light office skills and abilities from her assorted jobs but couldn't focus on anything that might be helpful. Her fear and borderline depression kept her in a place – until the day she made a choice, a decision. She was going to do whatever it took to support herself and take herself out of the fear that held her back. She had to. That's when she began to take stock of where she was. The "why's" of how she got there simply didn't matter anymore. That was just too much "navel gazing" and way too painful.

What am I good at doing, what do I love to do?

Goals allow you to control the direction of change in your favor.

– BRIAN TRACY

We all need to step back, take stock and start to analyze where we were, where we are and what we are going to do about tomorrow. But first, let's just get spontaneous. Just write a free-form thought list – no matter how irrelevant your ideas might be. Later, we can take our time, sort out our thoughts, dreams, ideas and visions. It doesn't have to be done within any kind of time frame – or does it? Anyway, let's just do it. Later, when our minds are fresh and clear, we can review. Sure, some of those things are impossible or impractical; but each of them has a grain of truth that can, and maybe should, be explored.

Gloria

Gloria took stock of where she was, what she could do, what she loved to do and what she wanted to do to get to the goal of supplementing their income. She reached into herself and came up with several things from her past, some of which overlapped what she could do and what she loved to do. After some serious consideration, she came up with a plan.

The items that stood out to her were the things that she loved, and made her happy, that she could drop in a second, whenever Matt needed her. Baking, knitting, crocheting; she could do something with these. What was her next step to be? Baking was out of the question. Baked goods needed attention that might not be available. Needlework. That was just the thing. She could knit or crochet baby blankets to sell. They could be done quickly. Craft shows were out of her comfort zone and her need to be at home made them impossible to attend, so websites like Etsy, eBay or Amazon just might work. Of course, there were others, but these were the ones with which Gloria and Matt felt most comfortable.

Ted

After some time and a lot of thought, Ted began to relax and then realized that all was not lost. He down-sized his home and made it wheelchair accessible and functional. With some of his retirement savings, he paid it off so that the only expenses he had would be for medical and insurance plans plus daily living expenses. For transportation, he was able to purchase a van, modify it and then learned how to drive it using only his hands.

Ted knew that he had skills and abilities that he could use to help others. In his chosen field of engineering, he used a lot of math, did a lot of research. He had done some teaching with his job and had enjoyed the work. He could use his skills as an engineer and researcher to help improve the lives of those who needed it. Where could he go next?

Maggie

Having been self-employed her entire adult life, Maggie decided to expand her own company and hire a few women who could take her place and whom she could train to do the job well. She could supervise with the best of them and Maggie knew that her hands-on policies were sure to lead her to success. Her daughter was willing and able to help her with the books for the present time. Now that she had a plan, what could she do and where could she go next to implement it?

Chris

Chris went downstairs to his basement and rummaged through the boxes his kids left behind when they moved on to adulthood. Aha! He found some of those little wooden toys he'd made and decided they would be great templates for others. He took stock of his assortment of woodworking tools, listed those needing repair and those needing to be replaced or added; and then he cleaned out and organized his garage to make room for a work shop.

Jessie

Jessie's self-assessment led to her looking for work where the assorted experiences of her background were an asset, not a liability. She was truly fearful, but she had no choice. She absolutely had to do something. Then, she realized that her abilities to research, organize and prioritize were valuable. Adding those to her office skills helped her to search for the work she was skilled and able to do, and she got help in putting together a cover letter and resume. She wasn't yet at the place where part time or hobbies would be enough to support her.

How can I turn this into a second career? …or do I even want one?

Give your thoughts over to the things that possess them, then follow your heart.

- JOY HOLLAND

What needs to happen for us to plan our new future? What research must be done to see our dreams turn into reality? Who can we connect with to help us? There is an answer for each of these questions and those answers depend on which direction and what is most feasible for us. The hardest part of this is the mental conditioning we must do; so that we can be open to any possibility that might be hiding in our past. In other words, how do we get there from here?

Gloria

Gloria could still work part time while Matt was able to care for himself somewhat. She purchased her supplies and pattern books from an online supplier with some of the savings from her retirement. She started to make the baby blankets in her spare time and began to build a stock so that when she needed to bring in an income and began to advertise, she'd have something to sell. Posting items on craft sites allowed her flexibility rather than trying to sell at craft shows. She also decided to make custom designed blankets for clients and considered making baby sweaters and booties. That would depend on customer requests.

She researched the companies where she wanted to advertise online and found that there was a cost to post her items. Hmmm, well then, she could do that. Meanwhile, she connected with a friend who was a web designer. He would build her a beautiful site and show her how to market herself and her baby blankets on it.

Gloria had found her niche and began to

enjoy what her future, and Matt's, would bring. They were beginning to feel safe and secure, knowing that what they had couldn't be taken from them because they weren't working for someone else. All things considered, their retirement income would be supplemented, not generously, but comfortably.

Ted

Ted did some research with the numerous local colleges and lined up a job as a tutor for struggling students. As the work was sporadic, he volunteered with the local SCORE group to help those who had or wanted to start a small business.

He started a blog to use as a catharsis and found that he reached many in his position that he could never have done had he not been writing. From his blog, he also lined up a contract to write his memoirs for quite a nice compensation.

Ted was rewarded in more than one way. Certainly, he had monetary income, but he also had the satisfaction of knowing that he could reach others and help them in ways that might have seemed impossible before. He turned his anger into something productive and positive and was able to make plans for the income he was going to be generating. He found peace within himself and was finally becoming content.

Maggie

Maggie put together a business plan and asked a member of SCORE to review and suggest changes/corrections/updates so that she could start out the right way. She picked out a name for her company and purchased needed equipment and supplies for a team of four and started out small. As the business grew, she'd be able to add to her teams. Maggie would train her team leaders from her first team and would give them guidance in picking out their own teams.

She advertised for help and had a teenager deliver flyers that had been designed especially for her, to various neighborhoods.

Since her clients had given her glowing references, she was comfortable in her ability to provide the best service possible. Also, since she'd been very good at organizing she advertised those skills and expanded her company's line. When the time came, she also had a website built that would provide leads for building her business and expanding her company.

Well on her way to a successful second career gave Maggie a new lease on life; and she discovered the joy in passing on what she knew to others, who would carry on what she considered to be her legacy.

Chris

For supplies, Chris still had contacts in the construction world and knew that there were always scraps of wood that would be thrown away in every construction job. His time was his own and he just wanted to keep busy. He contacted social services and asked if there was any reason he couldn't provide these toys to foster children at Christmas.

Permission granted, he connected with his former teams and, with his former co-workers, arranged to pick up what scraps he could use in making his toys. They were happy to toss them into a box to get them out of the way.

He knew he couldn't compete with the imports, but that wasn't important to him. Besides, weren't his toys far better quality than some of the junk that was imported? There was very little overhead because most of his raw materials were free for the taking.

This gave him something to do with his hands and out from under his loving wife's feet every day; plus, he gained the satisfaction of bringing a small measure of happiness to others. Chris began to build an impressive stock of toys to provide for the less fortunate and he was happy.

Jessie

Jessie was able to find and move into a small affordable apartment, where close by, she saw a huge office complex. She just knew that's where she was going to work. She discovered that there was to be a work fair at that location to be held two weeks following her move into the apartment. She took several copies of her resume and when she applied she was able to get an interview which resulted in another and then a job offer. She went to work for that major corporation where her skills and abilities were valued, and the opportunities opened.

With this new job, Jessie was able to stabilize her life, earn a decent income and improve her "lot in life." She still struggled with fear but with every new position she acquired, fear was reduced; until, after several years, it had almost completely disappeared. Jessie had found herself.

The Rest of the Story

A positive attitude will overcome reluctance to explore.

– JOY HOLLAND

Gloria

Gloria and Matt had seen several really good years together before Matt had another stroke and then a heart attack. That's when Gloria found herself alone. She took time to heal and grieve with her family, as well as with some of the connections she had made – other widows. She was eventually able to continue with her business. She'd made friends in her support group and found herself in the midst of activities that she really enjoyed; and continued to make new friends. She began to love life again and learned to have fun.

Ted

Ted was able to reach those who were struggling with various subjects. Through his own way of tutoring, which he modified according to needs and learning styles of each of his students, he found success. Along the way he helped them make life affirming choices for themselves. He found that interacting with those young people helped him reassess his own values and improved his outlook.

Out of the group of people he reached on his blog, he was able to make some of them friends and surprised himself with a new girlfriend, whom he later married.

He became grateful for his life and contentment settled within him which overcame the bitterness he'd previously experienced.

Maggie

Maggie learned just how good she was at teaching. Not only did she run her business well and see it expand, she was able to start another business, an off-shoot of her cleaning business, showing home owners how to organize for maximum efficiency – without it being a nightmare to keep going.

The number of her cleaning teams was growing and providing a comfortable income for all of them. Her daughter had gone on to build her own life; but by then, Maggie was able to afford a bookkeeper and accountant.

Chris

Chris enjoyed his woodworking so much so that he decided, as well as making toys, he'd build furniture. He contracted with a lumber yard for quality wood at good prices as well as finishing supplies. He found a partner who did the finish work, painting, staining and sealing the wood, who was also very good at marketing.

They managed to build quite a profitable business together selling custom furniture along with the toys. It was so successful that they had to lease a larger space for the work and a showroom for the furniture.

Jessie

Jessie worked for many years in the corporate world with that same company. She was content and managed to learn a little something about investing so that she could build herself a decent retirement income. She was also able to take time for her hobbies, reading, writing and cooking. She opened herself up enough to make new friends.

She also had acquired enough confidence to move out of state, on her own, and create a new life for herself; and she too found a new life companion and married.

Conclusion

Now, not many of us have been put into situations like the ones above; but we've all found ourselves at a loss of some kind or another. Most of us, at least, have options that those five might not have had. They were presented as examples of what can be done in various circumstances. But they all used the same format to move forward.

Here's the format they used, as a help for you – to pin down your future:

Ideas - just brainstorm and write down everything you can think of, you can edit later.

Dreams - what made you happy as a child? What were the dreams you had growing up?

If you can remember, what suggestions did friends, teachers, coaches, parents have? Again, write now, edit later.

Likes/Loves - what kinds of things did you like or really love to do? (No, teasing a sibling doesn't count!) Follow the same routine, write then edit.

Skills - what can you do? Include everything you can think of that you can do whether it might be job/career, family, sports, hobbies, whatever.

Opportunities - write down what you might consider potential opportunities. Look for ways that you can fill a need.

Start with your primary lists and narrow them down, combine items that seem to be alike. Once that's been accomplished, research the feasibility of each group.

- Will you need an investor or partner?

- What about ground floor expense – supplies, equipment etc.?

- Are there any zoning restrictions?

- Do you need a different location?

- What about potential future employees?
  - Will you/they need training?

- Is a license required?

- What about insurance?

- Have you considered any limitations?
  - Will you be able to work at your own pace?
  - Are there hurdles to implementation?
  - Can you overcome them?

- What can be done to make it a reality?

There are resources in abundance on the internet, with SCORE, KIBS and with your local Chamber of Commerce. What about YouTube?

It's an unlimited resource! Amazon is a treasure trove of books for research, some of them are used and can be bought for a song. Some of them are electronic, which I don't recommend because they cannot be copied or written in the margins. (I know they can be, but it's awkward to get to what you need quickly.)

Sometimes a new direction in education is necessary. Your local community college is a very good resource. There are also employment agencies that can guide you toward your goals. Senior Centers can be a valuable resource in guiding you. Many of them get jobs to post– if that's what you'd be interested in investigating.

The following is a very short list of suggestions that you may not have considered:

Memory Joggers	Ideas	Resources
Accounting	Any field	
Acting	Modeling/commercials	
Archeology		
Art	Painting/sculpture	
Audible Books	Read/Record	
Baking	Cookies/pies/cakes	
Baskets	Cookie/flower/candy/ toys	
Bed & Breakfast		
Ceramics/pottery		
Childcare		
Cleaning	Houses/offices	
Computer	Maintenance/set up etc.	
Coupon books	Compile 25 +/-	Contact local small business to sell coupons for small charge
Cooking	Gift meals	
Crafts		
Day Care	Children/Seniors	
Decorating	Rooms/homes	
Delivery service	Office lunches/snacks	Take orders/ delivery
Direct sales/home business		
Editing	Books/articles	

Elderly	Care/food/ medications/ companionship	
Fishing/hunting	Guide?	
Garden	Build/teach/grow/sell	
Graphics		
Hospital	Visit/Rock Babies	
House sitting	With/without pets	Some agents need this service
Journaling		
Invention	Find a need?	
Needlework	Knit/Crochet/ Embroidery/	
Organizing	Home/Office	
Personal Trainer		
Pet sitting	Dog Walker	
Politics	Volunteer/ Correspondence	
Proof Reading		
Real Estate	Sales/Appraiser/Closer/ Stage	
Repairs	Furniture/small appliances	
Retail	Sales/office	
Senior Centers	Visit/Gifts	
Sewing	Clothes/Alterations/ toys	
Teach/Mentor/ Coach	Academics/Sports/ Crafts/Home Arts	
Tourist Guide	Local Sights	
Web Design		

Woodworking		
Potential Issues:		
Licensing		
Permissions	HOA's	
Regulations	City/State	
Marketing		
Insurance	Product/Office/ Building	
Location	Rent/Lease/Buy	
SCORE		Counselors to America's Business (originated for Seniors in 1964)
KIBS		Knowledge Intensive Business Services

About the author

She's a combination of interests, abilities, experiences, cultures and families. Born into a military family, she spent her entire childhood moving around the country and lived overseas in England as a young child. Experienced in the "find a need and meet it" school of upbringing in a very large family; as the first born she found herself learning to become very resourceful. She married a military man and those skills became quite useful in rearing her own family.

Some of the reasons, including moving frequently and traumas in her childhood and teen years, she lost more jobs in her first three decades than most people had in a lifetime;

among them were baby sitter, office/file/ payroll clerk, bookkeeper, typist, retail/direct sales, receptionist, cashier, collector, program developer, administrative assistant, etc... She was alternately applauded, criticized, brow-beaten, harassed (once, literally chased around a desk), ignored, and mentored in various jobs. During those years she organized offices, developed a way to track collection income and print out necessary management reports for a bank, set up electronic means to track production for a clothing manufacturer, researched trucking archives, authored an employee manual and developed a reference manual for rehab health workers.

Through these experiences, or maybe because of them, the idea for this book was born. She realized that those in her time of life (retired or bordering on retirement, regardless of the circumstances), some with no way to support themselves, many with a life similar to her own, or those just looking to fill expanses of time, needed to have some way to fulfil that goal.

Thus, this book was written. None of the stories written here are based on person, alive or deceased. Those written about in this book are a complete figment of imagination.

Lightning Source UK Ltd.
Milton Keynes UK
UKHW011911290621
386378UK00007B/334/J

9 781664 227132